Russian Romantic Rep...

Romantische russische Klavierliteratur
Le Répertoire romantique de Russie

LEVEL 1

SELECTED AND EDITED BY STEPHEN COOMBS

 FABER **ff** MUSIC

7-95

CONTENTS

© 1998 by Faber Music Ltd
First Published in 1998 by Faber Music Ltd
3 Queen Square London WC1N 3AU
Cover design by S & M Tucker
Cover picture shows *St Basil's Cathedral and the monument
to Minin and Pojarsky on Red Square* (1852) by Iossif Weiss
Music processed by Chris Hinkins
French translation by Traduction Faber Music
German translation by Dorothee Göbel
Printed in England by Halstan & Co Ltd
All rights reserved

ISBN 0-571-51893-1

To buy Faber Music publications or to find out about the full range of titles available
please contact your local music retailer or Faber Music sales enquiries:

Tel: +44 (0)1279 82 89 82
Fax: +44 (0)1279 82 89 83
E-mail: sales@fabermusic.co.uk
Website://www.fabermusic.co.uk

INTRODUCTION

In the field of piano repertoire, Russian music holds a special place. The sheer number and diversity of works is astounding; moreover, the quality of imagination it exhibits, together with the accomplishment of the piano-writing itself, is of the highest standard. Yet, although the piano music of Tchaikovsky, Rakhmaninov, Skryabin and Prokofiev is today regularly performed in concert halls throughout the world, the vast majority of the piano works by their teachers and contemporaries is hardly known at all. There was a staggering amount of excellent piano music written in Russia during the latter part of the nineteenth century – an extraordinary situation when you consider that the first Russian music to have any wider influence or significance was written by a man whose sister died as recently as 1906. That man was Mikhail Glinka (1804-1857) and it was his pioneering efforts that shaped the future of Russian piano music.

Glinka was not a professional musician and his music was written to entertain in the drawing-room rather than impress in the concert hall. He was, however, a fine pianist and his many small-scale piano works (mazurkas, waltzes and salon pieces with descriptive titles) became the model for many later Russian composers. Unlike the German school, which naturally created large-scale works by developing small melodic ideas against a larger tonal scheme, the Russians concentrated on strong melodic statement and subsequent variation. The result is a large number of piano miniatures that display a vivid musical imagination and an attention to texture.

Because of the extremely provincial aspect of Russian musical life in the early nineteenth century, Western music was mainly the preserve of rich amateurs. There was no formal training available in Russia itself and to compensate for this, the first Russian composers shared their knowledge, gained largely abroad, freely among themselves. This led, in turn, to a remarkable form of artistic cross-fertilisation; almost all the Russian composers of the nineteenth century received advice and instruction from their colleagues and friends. Glinka, who had studied in Berlin, lent his note books containing all the substance of his lessons abroad to Alexander Dargomïzhsky (1813-1869) whose place in the history of Russian music became second only to Glinka. Glinka also helped and influenced Mily Balakirev (1837-1910) who gave advice and help to Pyotr Ilyich Tchaikovsky (1840-1893). Tchaikovsky's pronouncement that 'Glinka's *Kamarinskay* was the acorn which grew into the oak of Russian music' was no empty rhetoric. Indeed, Tchaikovsky's first masterpiece, his *Romeo and Juliet* overture, shows some striking similarities to sections of Glinka's opera *Ruslan and Lyudmila*.

In the second half of the nineteenth century a new conflict arose among the next generation of Russian composers. By 1865, the Russian musical establishment was dominated by the opposing figures of Balakirev and Anton Rubinstein (1829-1894). Though both paid homage to the earlier composer Glinka, they disagreed about the direction Russian music should take. Rubinstein looked to the west for inspiration (most particularly to Germany). Balakirev, on the other hand, looked towards the east and Russia's own heritage of folksong and ethnic diversity. Eventually Balakirev's views came to influence a whole generation of composers. The rhythms and inflections of folk music began to appear, together with an imaginative and colourful harmony more suited to the modal scales found in folksong. Russian music began to have a new and distinctive voice.

Balakirev went on to teach and influence Alexander Borodin (1833-1887), César Cui (1835-1918), Modest Musorgsky (1839-1881) and Nikolay Rimsky-Korsakov (1844-1908). Rimsky-Korsakov proved to be another remarkable teacher, whose pupils included Anatol Lyadov (1855-1914), Anton Arensky (1861-1906), Felix Blumenfeld (1863-1931), Alexander Glazunov (1865-1936), Alexander Kopïlov (1854-1911) and Nikolay Amani (1872-1904). By the end of the century, dozens of new composers were writing vast amounts of music – much of it for the piano. Arensky's pupils included Sergey Rakhmaninov (1873-1943) and Alexander Skryabin (1872-1915), – Skryabin also studied with Tchaikovsky's student Alexander Taneyev (1856-1915) who in turn taught Sergey Liapunov (1859-1924) and Alexy Stanchinsky (1888-1914). Of the composers featured in these volumes, only Alexander Il'yinsky (1859-1920), Khvoshchinsky (dates unknown) and Vladimir Rebikov (1866-1920) have no direct connection with the above composers, although Rebikov was a student of Tchaikovsky's pupil Nikolay Klenovsky (1857-1915).

Strangely, much of this music remained unknown outside Russia and after the Russian revolution most of it disappeared completely. It is hard to explain why this should have happened though, undoubtedly, the speed with which Russian music developed played a part in its eventual neglect. By the time the west became aware of this rich repertoire, in the early years of the twentieth century, the Russian avant-garde was already beginning to attract the attention of the world. By 1912, Stravinsky had already given the premières of his ballets *The Firebird* and *Petrushka* and was now at work on *The Rite of Spring*, whilst back at the St Petersburg Conservatory Lyadov's brilliant pupil Sergey Prokofiev had won the Rubinstein Prize with his First Piano Concerto. With the 1917 Revolution the old Imperial Russia, together with the creative expression of it, was swept aside.

Today there is a greater interest in this romantic piano repertoire, though unfortunately it is still very difficult, or impossible, to find copies of much of the music. I hope this collection will serve as an introduction to some fascinating music and although is is not possible to include every composer who figured in Russian musical life, I have tried to give a representative selection of composers and works that I believe deserve to be better known.

All fingering and pedal markings are intended as suggestions only. Every piece in this volume has been chosen, primarily, because of the quality of the music and every pianist whether performer, teacher, student or general music-lover will, I hope, find much to delight and surprise them.

Stephen Coombs, October 1998

EINLEITUNG

Die Werke russischer Komponisten haben einen besonderen Stellenwert im Klavierrepertoire. Schon allein die Anzahl und Vielseitigkeit der Werke ist bewundernswert, überdies entsprechen musikalische Inspiration und kunstvoller Klaviersatz höchsten Ansprüchen. Und dennoch kennt man die wenigsten Klavierwerke der Lehrer und Zeitgenossen von Tschaikowsky, Rachmaninow, Skrjabin und Prokofjew, deren Werke heute in Konzertsälen auf der ganzen Welt gespielt werden. Gegen Ende des 19. Jahrhunderts entstand in Rußland eine geradezu verblüffende Fülle hervorragender Klavierwerke. Dies ist eine außergewöhnliche Konstellation gerade angesichts der Tatsache, daß russische Musik von größerer Bedeutung oder Nachwirkung von jemandem komponiert wurde, dessen Schwester erst 1906 starb. Es handelt sich um Michail Glinka (1804-1857), dessen wegweisende Bemühungen die Entwicklung russischer Klaviermusik prägten.

Glinka war kein Berufsmusiker; seine Werke sollten eher in den Salons unterhalten denn im Konzertsaal große Wirkung machen. Er war allerdings ein guter Pianist, und seine zahlreichen kleinen Klavierwerke (Mazurken, Walzer und Charakterstücke) dienten vielen späteren russischen Komponisten zum Vorbild. Im Gegensatz zu den an deutscher Tradition orientierten Komponisten, die durch Verarbeitung kurzer melodischer Gedanken innerhalb eines tonal bestimmten Rahmens umfangreiche Werke schufen, konzentrierten sich die russischen Komponisten auf starke melodische Einfälle und deren Variation. So entstanden zahlreiche Klavierminiaturen, die durch lebhafte musikalische Inspiration und eine sorgfältig ausgearbeitete Satztechnik geprägt sind.

Da das Musikleben Rußlands im frühen 19. Jahrhundert nur wenig entwickelt war, bedeutete die Beschäftigung mit westlicher Kunstmusik vor allem ein Privileg vermögender Musikliebhaber. Um dem Mangel abzuhelfen, daß es in Rußland selber keinerlei Ausbildungsmöglichkeiten gab, tauschten sich die ersten russischen Komponisten, die ihre Kenntnisse primär im Ausland erworben hatten, untereinander intensiv aus. Dies führte zu einer bemerkenswerten künstlerischen Befruchtung; fast alle russischen Komponisten des 19. Jahrhunderts wurden durch Freunde und Kollegen unterwiesen und konnten auf deren Rat in künstlerischen Fragen setzen. Glinka, der in Berlin studiert hatte, lieh Alexander Dargomischky (1813-1869) seine Notizbücher, die alles umfaßten, was er im Ausland gelernt hatte. In der Geschichte der russischen Musik wird die Bedeutung Dargomischkys nur durch Glinka selber überboten. Glinka beriet und beeinflußte auch Mili Balakirew (1837-1910), der wiederum Ratschläge und Empfehlungen an Tschaikowsky (1840-1893) weitergab. Tschaikowskys Diktum, "daß Glinkas *Kamarinskaja* die Zukunft der russischen sinfonischen Musik in sich wie eine Eichel die Eiche berge", war keine leere Worthülse. Tschaikowskys erstes Meisterwerk, seine Ouvertüre *Romeo und Julia*, zeigt in der Tat einige erstaunliche Verwandtschaften mit Abschnitten aus Glinkas Oper *Ruslan und Ludmilla*.

In der zweiten Hälfte des 19. Jahrhunderts ergab sich unter der nächsten Generation russischer Komponisten ein neuer Konflikt. Um 1865 wurde die Musikwelt Rußlands durch die beiden gegensätzlichen Figuren Balakirew und Anton Rubinstein (1829-1894) geprägt. Obwohl beide sich auf den Komponisten Glinka beriefen, waren sie doch verschiedener Meinung über die Ziele russischer Musik. Während Rubinstein sich am Westen, vor allem an Deutschland orientierte, wandte Balakirew sich dagegen dem Osten und Rußlands Nationalerbe hinsichtlich Liedgut und ethnischer Vielfalt zu. Balakirews Ansichten sollten letztlich ganze Generation von Komponisten beeinflussen. Die Rythmen und Sprachmelodien der Volksmusik erschienen nun auch in der Kunstmusik, ergänzt durch eine phantasievolle und farbige Harmonik, die den modalen Skalen der Volksmusik eher entsprach. Russische Musik bekam allmählich einen neuen und ganz eigenen Charakter.

Balakirew unterrichtete und beeinflußte Alexander Borodin (1833-1887), César Cui (1835-1918), Modest Mussorgsky (1839-1881) und Nikolai Rimski-Korsakow (1844-1908). Rimski-Korsakow wiederum wurde zu einem ausgezeichneten Lehrer, zu dessen Schülern Anatol Lyadow (1855-1914), Anton Arensky (1861-1906), Felix Blumenfeld (1863-1931), Alexander Glasunow (1865-1936), Alexander Kopilow (1854-1911) und Nikolai Amani (1872-1904) gehörten. Zum Ende des Jahrhunderts hin schrieben Dutzende neuer Komponisten zahlreiche Werke, größtenteils für Klavier. Zu Arenskys Schülern gehörten Sergej Rachmaninow (1873-1943) und Alexander Skrjabin (1872-1915). Skrjabin wurde auch von dem Tschaikowsky-Schüler Alexander Taneyew (1856-1915) unterrichtet, der wiederum Sergej Ljapunow (1859-1924) und Alexej Stanschinsky (1888-1914) unterwies. Unter den in dieser Sammlung vorgestellten Komponisten haben nur Alexander Iljinsky (1859-1920), Kwostschinsky (Daten nicht bekannt) und Vladimir Rebikow (1866-1920) keine direkte Verbindung zu den obengenannten Komponisten; Rebikow allerdings war über seinen Lehrer Nikolai Klenowsky (1857-1915) ein Enkelschüler von Tschaikowsky.

Merkwürdigerweise blieb vieles aus diesem Repertoire außerhalb Rußlands unbekannt, und das meiste geriet nach der Oktoberrevolution in Vergessenheit. Warum das geschah, läßt sich schwer nachvollziehen, allerdings hat zweifellos das Tempo, in dem sich die russische Musik weiterentwickelte, hierbei eine Rolle gespielt. Als der Westen in den frühen Jahren des 20. Jahrhunderts auf dieses reiche Repertoire aufmerksam wurde, begann schon die russische Avantgarde das Interesse der Welt auf sich zu lenken. 1912 hatte Strawinsky schon seine Ballette *Feuervogel* und *Petruschka* uraufgeführt und arbeitete an *Le sacre du printemps*, während Sergej Prokofjew, der herausragende Schüler von Lyadow, im Konservatorium von St. Petersburg mit seinem ersten Klavierkonzert den Rubinstein-Preis gewonnen hatte. Das alte kaiserliche Rußland und seine eigene Kunstsprache wurden dann im Zuge der Oktoberrevolution 1917 hinweggefegt.

Heute stößt dieses Repertoire romantischer Klaviermusik wieder auf größeres Interesse, obwohl es immer noch sehr schwierig oder auch unmöglich ist, Notenausgaben zu finden. Ich hoffe, daß diese Sammlung als Einführung in dieses faszinierende Repertoire dienen kann. Obwohl es nicht möglich war, jeden Komponisten, der im russischen Musikleben eine Rolle spielte, in die Sammlung aufzunehmen, so habe ich doch versucht, eine repräsentative Auswahl solcher Komponisten und Werke zu geben, die meines Erachtens Aufmerksamkeit verdienen.

Fingersätze und Hinweise zum Pedalgebrauch sind lediglich als Vorschläge anzusehen. Die hier vorgestellten Werke wurden vor allem nach ihrer musikalischen Qualität ausgewählt, und ich hoffe, daß jeder Klavierspieler, sei er nun künstlerisch tätig, sei er Lehrer, Student oder Musikliebhaber, in diesen Werken Überraschendes und Begeisterndes finden möge.

Stephen Coombs, Oktober 1998

INTRODUCTION

La musique russe occupe une place à part dans le répertoire pour piano. Ses œuvres, étonnamment nombreuses et diversifiées, font montre d'une qualité d'imagination et d'une écriture pianistique de la plus haute teneur. Pourtant, et bien que les œuvres pour piano de Tchaïkovski, Rachmaninov, Scriabine et Prokofiev soient aujourd'hui régulièrement interprétées dans les salles de concert du monde entier, la grande majorité des pièces pour piano de leurs maîtres et contemporains sont à peine connues. Un nombre astronomique d'excellentes pièces pour piano furent écrites en Russie dans la seconde moitié du XIXᵉ siècle – une situation extraordinaire lorsque l'on songe que la première musique russe à avoir eu une grande influence ou importance fut composée par un homme, Mikhail Glinka (1804-1857), dont la sœur ne mourut qu'en 1906 et dont les efforts novateurs façonnèrent l'avenir de la musique pour piano russe.

Glinka, musicien non professionnel, composa une musique davantage destinée à divertir dans les salons qu'à impressionner dans les salles de concert. Mais il était bon pianiste et ses nombreuses œuvres pianistiques à petite échelle (mazurkas, valses et pièces de salon aux titres descriptifs) devinrent un modèle pour quantité de compositeurs russes ultérieurs. Contrairement à l'école allemande, qui produisit naturellement des œuvres à grande échelle en développant de petites idées mélodiques contre un schéma tonal plus ample, les Russes s'attachèrent à une énonciation mélodique forte et aux variations subséquentes. Ce qui se traduisit par un grand nombre de miniatures pour piano dotées d'une imagination musicale vive et d'une texture soignée.

Étant donné le caractère extrêmement provincial de la vie musicale russe au début du XIXᵉ siècle, la musique occidentale fut surtout l'apanage de riches amateurs. Aucune formation officielle n'existait en Russie, manque auquel les premiers compositeurs russes pallièrent en partageant librement leurs connaissances, en grande partie acquises à l'étranger. Ce qui suscita, en retour, une remarquable forme de croisement artistique: presque tous les compositeurs russes du XIXᵉ siècle reçurent conseils et enseignements de leurs collègues et amis. Glinka, qui avait étudié à Berlin, prêta ainsi ses carnets – dépositaires de toute la substance de ses leçons à l'étranger – à Alexandre Dargomijski (1813-1869), qui occupa la deuxième place (juste derrière Glinka) dans l'histoire de la musique russe de l'époque. Glinka aida également, et influença, Milij Balakirev (1837-1910), qui conseilla et aida Piotr Ilitch Tchaïkovski (1840-1893). La déclaration de Tchaïkovski: "*Kamarinskaïa* de Glinka fut le gland qui devint le chêne de la musique russe" ne fut pas vide rhétorique, le premier chef-d'œuvre de Tchaïkovski, son ouverture *Roméo et Juliette*, présentant de frappantes ressemblances avec des sections de l'opéra de Glinka, *Russlan et Ludmilla*.

Dans la seconde moitié du XIXᵉ siècle, un nouveau conflit divisa la génération suivante de compositeurs russes. En 1865, les figures antagonistes de Balakirev et d'Anton Rubinstein (1829-1894) dominaient le monde musical russe. Si tous deux rendaient hommage à leur aîné Glinka, ils étaient en désaccord quant à l'orientation à venir de la musique russe. Rubinstein rechercha l'inspiration du côté de l'Occident (tout particulièrement en Allemagne); Balakirev, a contrario, se tourna vers l'Orient, vers l'héritage des chansons populaires et de la diversité ethnique russes, influençant finalement toute une génération de compositeurs. Les rythmes et inflexions de la musique populaire apparurent bientôt, assortis d'une harmonie imaginative et colorée plus adaptée aux gammes modales des mélodies populaires. La musique russe commença de se doter d'une voix nouvelle et distinctive.

Balakirev enseigna et influença Alexandre Borodine (1833-1887), César Cui (1835-1918), Modeste Moussorgski (1839-1881) et Nikolaï Rimski-Korsakov (1844-1908) – lequel se révéla également un remarquable maître, qui compta parmi ses élèves Anatoli Liadov (1855-1914), Anton Arenski (1861-1906), Felix Blumenfeld (1863-1931), Alexandre Glazounov(1865-1936), Alexandre Kopilov (1854-1911) et Nicolaï Amani (1872-1904). À la fin du siècle, des dizaines de nouveaux compositeurs écrivirent quantité et quantité de pièces, essentiellement pour piano. Arenski eut, entre autres élèves, Sergueï Rachmaninov (1873-1943) et Alexander Scriabine (1872-1915) – lequel étudia aussi avec un élève de Tchaïkovski, Alexander Taneïev (1856-1915), qui enseigna à son tour Sergueï Liapounov (1859-1924) et Alexi Stanchinski (1888-1914). De tous les compositeurs présentés dans ces volumes, seuls Alexandre Iljinski (1859-1920), Khvoshchinski (dates inconnues) et Vladimir Rebikov (1866-1920) n'ont aucun lien direct avec les compositeurs susmentionnés – Rebikov étudia cependant auprès d'un élève de Tchaïkovski, Nicolaï Klenovski (1857-1915).

Curieusement, une grande partie de cette musique demeura inconnue hors de Russie et la plupart de ces pièces disparurent après la révolution russe. Il est difficile d'expliquer pareille disparition, même si la vitesse avec laquelle la musique russe se développa contribua indubitablement à cet abandon ultime. Lorsque l'Occident prit conscience de ce riche répertoire, au début du XXᵉ siècle, l'avant-garde russe commençait déjà à attirer l'attention du monde. En 1912, Stravinski, qui avait déjà donné le premières de ses ballets *L'Oiseau de feu* et *Pétrouchka*, travaillait au *Sacre du printemps*, tandis que, de retour au Conservatoire de Saint-Pétersbourg, le brillant élève de Liadov, Sergueï Prokofiev, venait de remporter le prix Rubinstein avec son Premier Concerto pour piano. La révolution de 1917 balaya la vieille Russie impériale et son expression créatrice.

De nos jours, ce répertoire pianistique bénéficie d'un regain d'intérêt, même s'il demeure malheureusement très difficile, voire impossible, de trouver des copies de nombreuses pièces. J'espère que la présente collection servira d'introduction à une musique fascinante et, bien qu'il soit exclu d'y faire figurer tous les acteurs de la vie musicale russe, j'ai tenté de proposer une sélection représentative des compositeurs et des œuvres qui, à mons sens, méritent d'être mieux connus.

Tous les doigtés et pédales ne se veulent que des suggestions. Chaque pièces de ce volume a été choisie avant tout pour la qualité de la musique et tout pianiste, qu'il soit interprète, professeur, étudiant ou simple mélomane, y trouvera, je l'espère, force matière à ravissement et surprise.

Stephen Coombs, octobre 1998

Mazurka
Op. 57 No. 3

A.K. Lyadov
(1855–1914)

On One Leg

A.A. Kopïlov
(1854–1911)

A Tear
(quasi Fantasia)

M.P. Musorgsky
(1839–81)

A Musical Snuffbox

V.I. Rebikov
(1866–1920)

Tempo di Valse

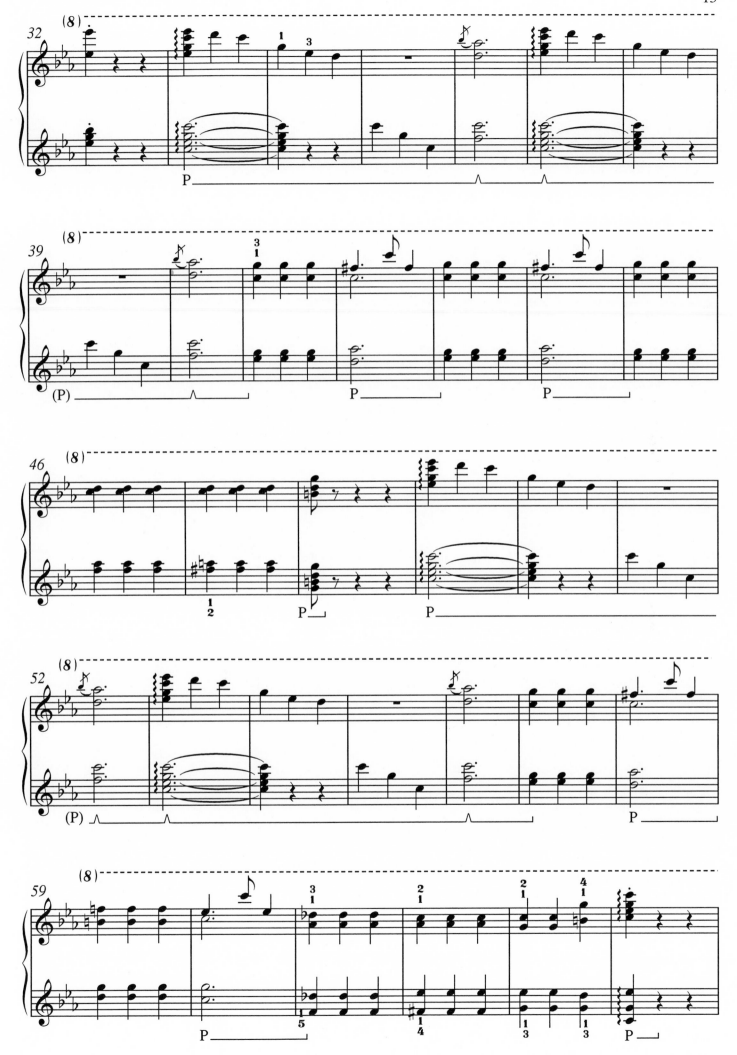

Intermezzo
Op. 1 No. 2

A.P. Borodin
(1833–87)

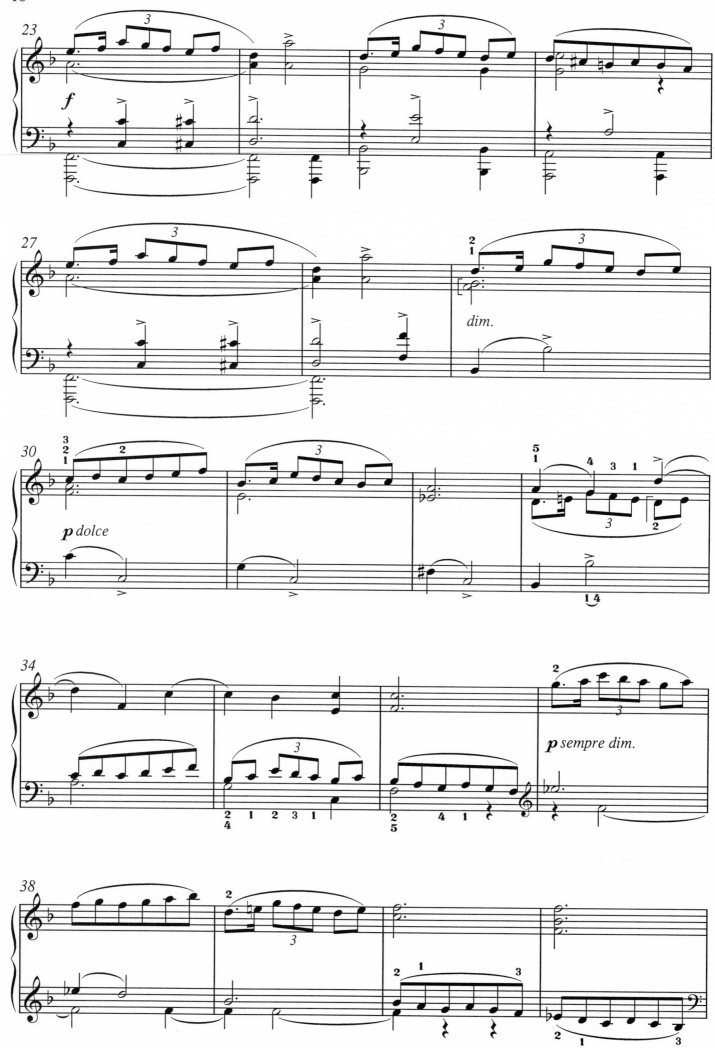

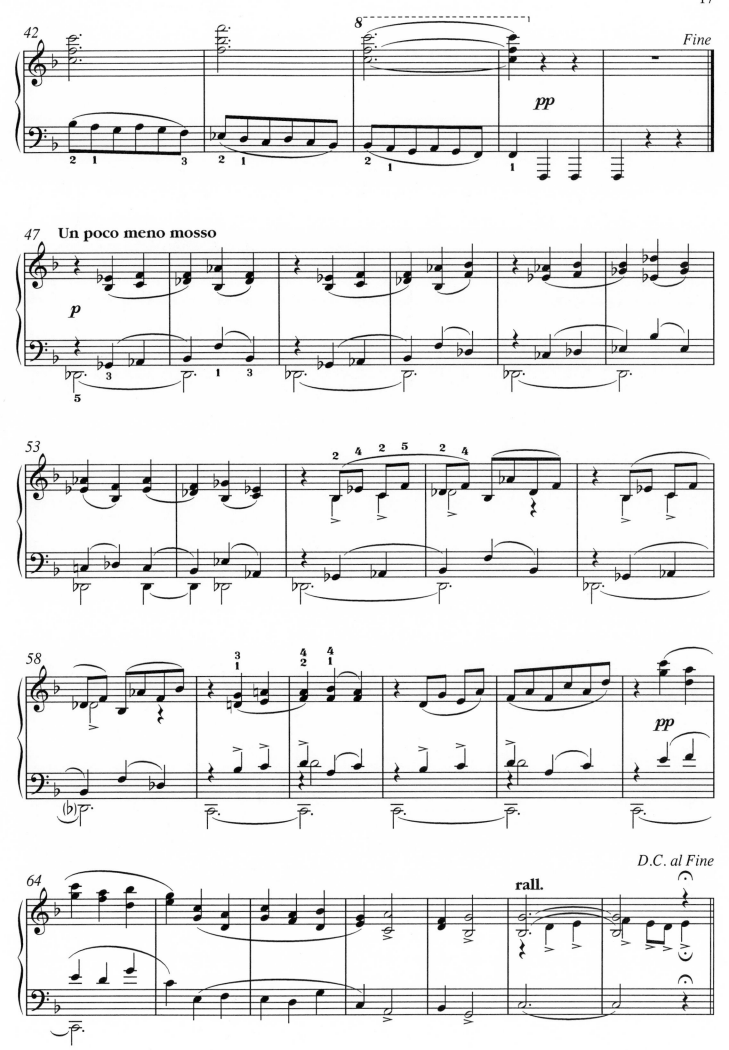

Sketch
Op. 1 No. 3

A.V. Stanchinsky
(1888–1914)

Prelude
Op. 36 No. 3

A.K. Lyadov
(1855–1914)

Mazurka

M.I. Glinka
(1804–57)

The Witch
Op. 39 No. 20

P.I. Tchaikovsky
(1840–93)

24

Prelude
Op. 17 No. 6

A.N. Skryabin
(1872–1915)

Andante doloroso

© 1998 by Faber Music Ltd.

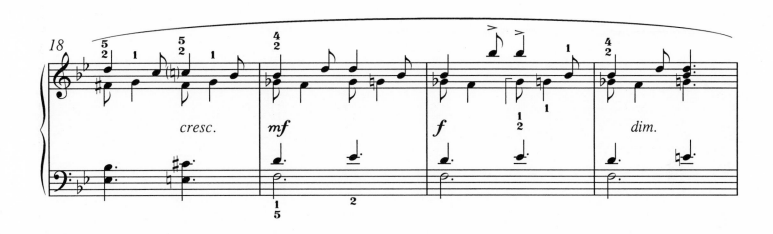

Mazurka
Op. 8 No. 1

P. Khvoshchinsky

Snuffbox Waltz

A.S. Dargomïzhsky
(1813–69)

Oriental Dance

Op. 2 No. 5

V.I. Rebikov
(1866–1920)

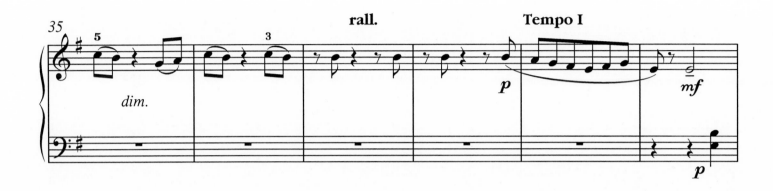

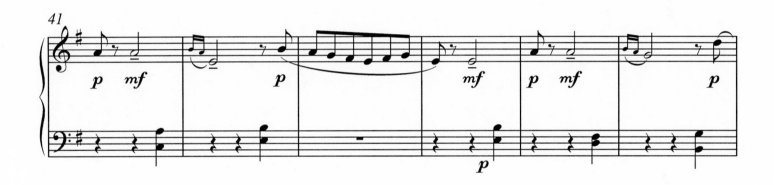

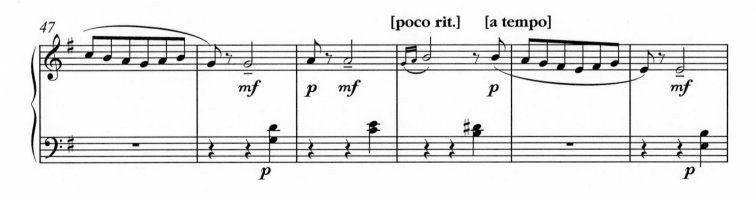

Berceuse
Op. 13 (from *Noure and Anitra Suite*)

A.A. Il'yinsky
(1859–1920)

Playing Ball
Op. 59 No.1

S.M. Lyapunov
(1859–1924)

Little Waltz
Op. 15 No. 2

N. Amani
(1872–1904)

Grimaces
Op. 64 No. 1

A.K. Lyadov
(1855–1914)

Farewell Waltz

M.I. Glinka
(1804–57)